PIANO • VOCAL • GUITAR

SELECTIONS FROM

THE MAN FROM SNOWY RIVER

T0058983

HAL•LEONARD®
CORPORATION

7777 W. BLUEMOUND RD. P.O. BOX 13819 MILWAUKEE, WI 53213

Visit Hal Leonard Online at
www.halleonard.com

SELECTIONS FROM

Contents

THE MAN FROM SNOWY RIVER

- It seemed like a bad idea at the time, the throwaway suggestion round a fire, late one night: "Why don't you make a film of "The Man From Snowy River"? Geoff Burrowes and George Miller's immediate reaction was to dismiss it. The poem, they believed, was too much a cliche in the Australian consciousness. But the more they thought, the more they realised that Banjo Paterson's epic poem was the chance to make a movie with a spectacular, heart-pounding climax unlike anything ever attempted in Australia. But how to get to that tremendous ending?

- At this moment of recognition the film's beginnings were a lot closer to its completion than they guessed. Two years before, in 1977, Burrowes and George Miller, probably Australia's leading television director, had made a documentary on the High Country horses, the men and the mountains that lie at the heart of the appeal of Paterson's poem. Together they understood this appeal better than any film makers alive. And the problem of getting a script to the point where the poem begins — "There was movement at the station" — wasn't such a problem when they realised that Paterson gave significant clues. Nuggets of information on the characters and their interaction that could be fashioned into a film that would push Australian cinema into a bigger dimension and a bold new direction.

- The story was waiting and the location was there — the Great Dividing Range, an awesome mountain immensity that few Australians and no overseas audience had seen on screen. All that was needed was the right casting and more cash than had ever been spent on an Australian movie.

- Again the solution to these problems was closer to realisation than Burrows and Miller could hope. The movie, they reckoned, would cost more than $1 million and to make money would have to gross big overseas.

- At that time millionaire entrepreneur Michael Edgley was 'out shopping' overseas on a buying spree that would cost him $15 million for a package that included "Barnum", Tommy Steele, Marcel Marceau and The Great Moscow Circus. And Edgley, Australia's biggest and most far sighted entrepreneur was, they knew, considering expanding into film and television.

- They were approached by Simon Wincer, an Edgley associate and himself a top producer and director. Wincer, and Edgley, grabbed at the idea.

- Now they had the backing of Michael Edgley International and an expanded team — but would it make money? To provide the film with an international stature they had to have an international "name". The snag was that they agreed, were adamant, that the lead role of "the man" had to go to an unknown, an actor young enough to fit Paterson's description of "a stripling" and with a face fresh to Australian audiences, one that they would think of as belonging to none but the Man From Snowy River.

- The twin problems of finding a name actor to sell the movie overseas and an unknown to give it legitimacy in Australia were solved by Tom Burlinson and Kirk Douglas.

- Burlingson was among the last of 2,000 young men considered for the part. Burlingson came to the audition "cold", not knowing what he was reading for, but within minutes of the screen test Miller, Burrowes and Wincer knew their search had ended. In the meantime, the name actor they wanted, like the story and the location of the film, was waiting on their doorstep. Kirk Douglas was in Australia for the 1980 Australian Film Awards.

- Sir Robert Helpman was also a guest at the awards. Helpman numbers many celebrities among his friends and he and Douglas struck up a quick rapport. Jack Thompson who was already cast as Clancy and had met Kirk at Cannes earlier in the year mentioned his own enthusiasm for the project. Kirk read the script and was interested.

- Here was an actor who had huge appeal for audiences around the world and a man who was eager to be part of the Australian film renaissance. Eager, but he had his price. By now the film's principals had unshaken belief in "Snowy" and upped the budget to $5 million.

- So they had two of the main roles cast. Burlingson as Jim Craig, "the man", and Douglas as Harrison, who owned the runaway colt. And they had a third part filled. Douglas, who offered many suggested changes to the script, came up with the idea of himself in a dual part as Harrison and his brother Spur.

- The rest of the casting fell naturally into place. Jack Thompson was Clancy the legend, it was as simple as that. And for the part of Jessica, Harison's daughter and the girl Jim Craig loves, they chose Sigrid Thornton. Wincer had directed her in his feature film "snapshot" and knew she was right for this role.

- They took these four and a dozen other actors to Merrijig, 220 kilometres from Melbourne at the foot of the Great Dividing Range. There they were joined by 90 horses and forty mountain men, grizzled, hard men who were dubbed with heavy irony "the Buttercup Bunch", but who rode like the Wild Bunch.

- On March 30, 1981, George Miller called for quiet on set and seven months later the film was in the can.

- It hadn't been such a bad idea after all.

• *BRUCE ROWLAND* •

Bruce's writing career started in 1964, writing arrangements for the "Go Show" - a teenage show on the 0/10 Network and then progressed to the children's show "Magic Circle Club" which became "Adventure Island" on the ABC. For these two shows he was writing ten songs per week - every week for five years!

Bruce moved into jingle writing in 1969 and wrote over 3,000 jingles, from dog food to airlines, and everything in-between - winning a Cleo Award for his Phillips music in 1978. He also wrote themes for Maquarie News - Terry Willesee - 3AW - 6KY - Newsworld - Rolf Harris Show and many more. Also background music for Zoo Family - Neighbours - Dolphin Bay and lots of others.

His score for "The Man From Snowy River" achieved Platinum status and is the highest selling film score in Australia. The second highest is "Phar Lap" which he also wrote.

Bruce's other credits include "All The Rivers Run" (1 and 11), "Now And Forever" (starring Cheryl Ladd), "Anzacs", "Backstage", "Cool Change", "Running From The Guns", "Rebel", "Snowy River 11", "Bushfire Moon", six cartoons for Hanna-Barbera (US), "Big Foot" for Walt Disney, "Harris Downunder" and "Bad Lands 2001" for Weintraub Corporation and a new Disney feature called "Cheetah And Friends".

Bruce won the AFI Award for Best Score in 1982 for "The Man From Snowy River"; in 1983 for "Pharlap" and in 1985 for "Rebel".

He is equally at home composing for large orchestras or all electronic and can tailor his budgets according to your requirements. He has also composed a considerable amount of work on fairlight and synclavier and has just finished a Rock 'N' Roll score for a new film titled "Depth Of Feeling".

He won a Melbourne Art Directors Award for his music in the "Australia" commercials in 1988.

In February 1990, he completed the score for the "Gunsmoke 11 - The Lost Apache" for CBS and turned out to be the highest rating MOR for the company for five years. In August 1990, he wrote the music for "Which Way Home", a three hour MOR for the Turner Network starring Cybil Shepherd.

In October 1990, Bruce also wrote "Fast Getaway" for Wasatch, an independent American feature starring Garry Halme.

BACK TO THE MOUNTAINS
(Mountain Theme II)

Composed and Arranged by
BRUCE ROWLAND

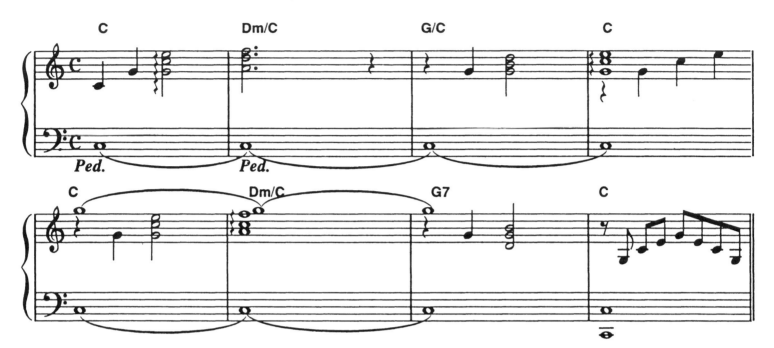

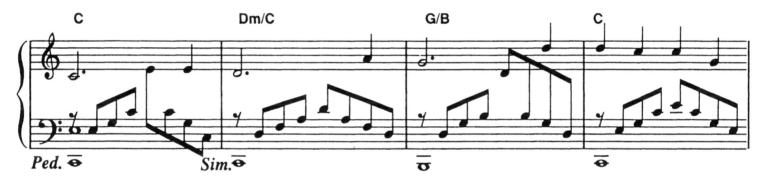

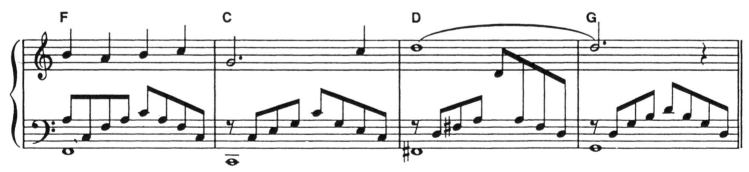

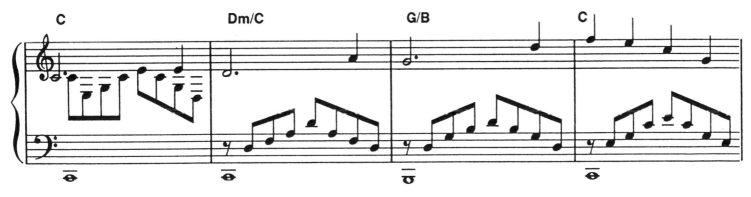

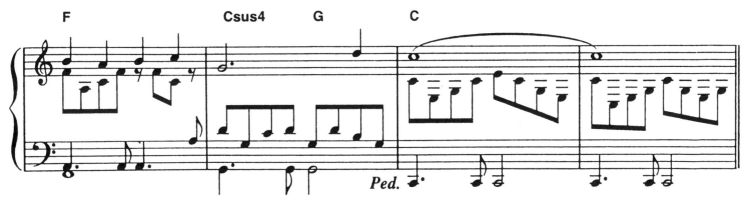

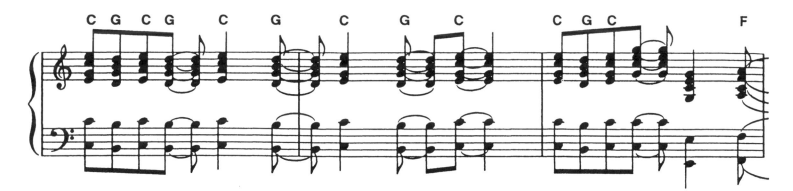

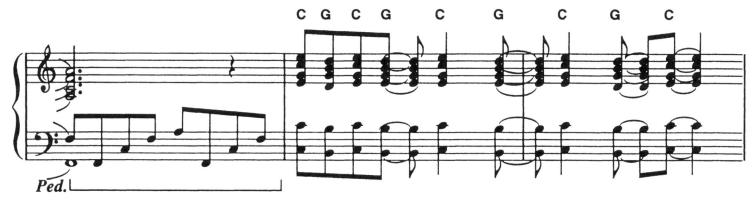

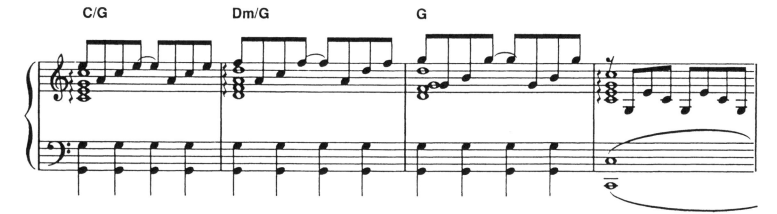

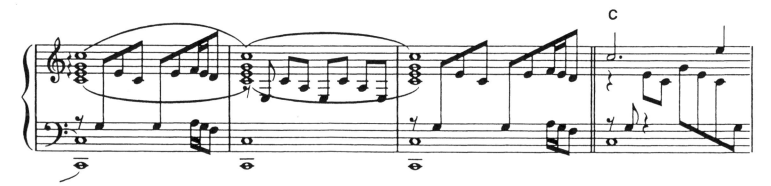

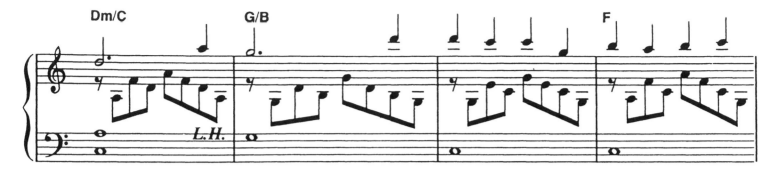

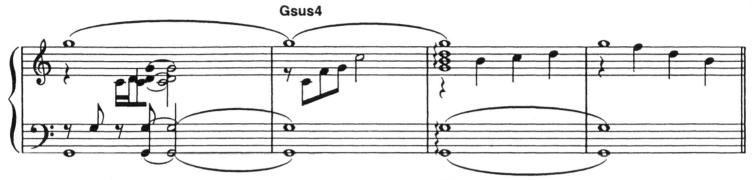

BY THE FIRESIDE

Composed and Arranged by
BRUCE ROWLAND

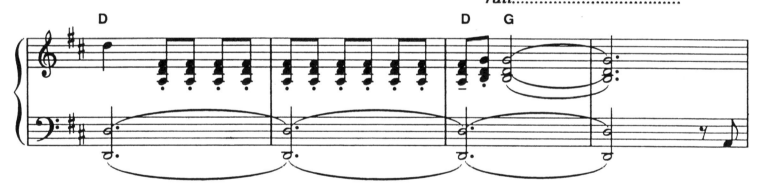

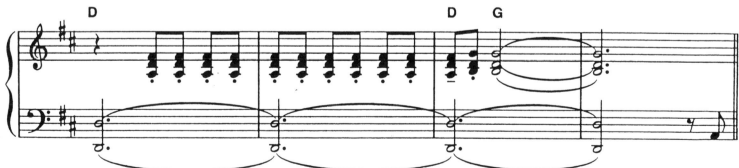

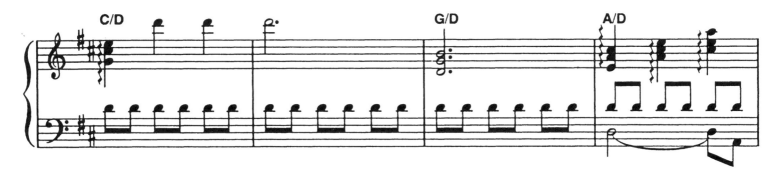

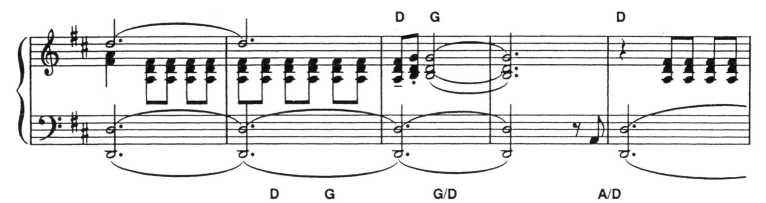

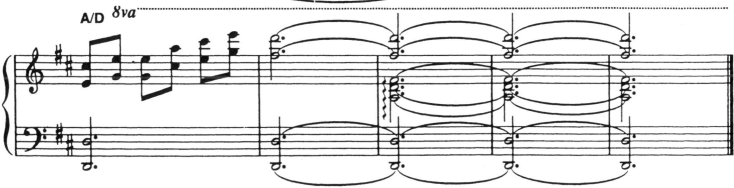

JESSICA'S THEME
(Breaking In The Colt)

Composed and Arranged by
BRUCE ROWLAND

Rubato — Allegro moderato

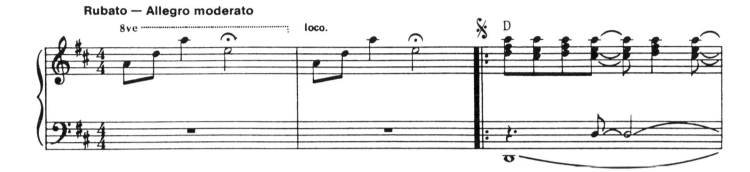

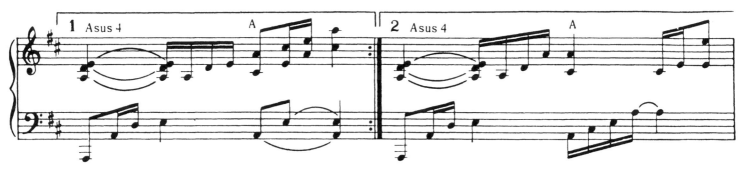

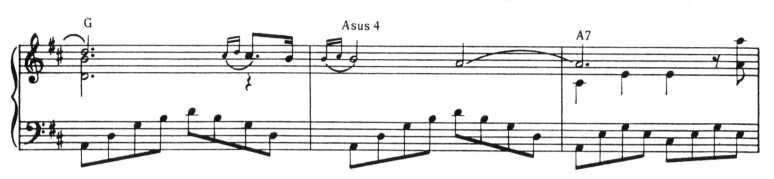

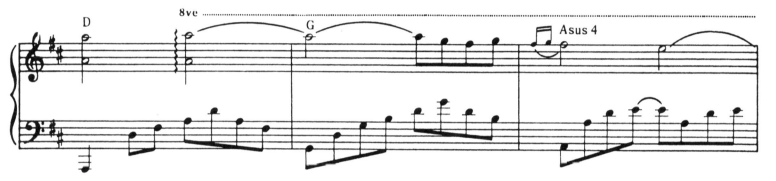

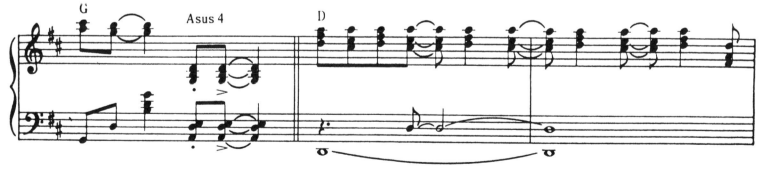

JESSICA'S SONATA NO. 2

Composed and Arranged by
BRUCE ROWLAND

to CODA⊕

Molto rubato

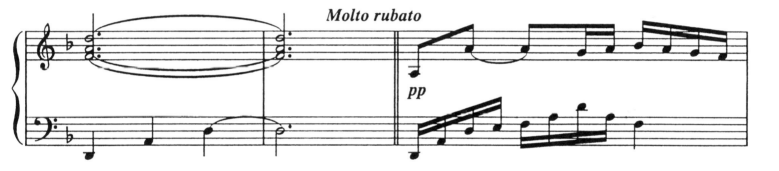

D.S.𝄋 al CODA⊕   ⊕CODA
Fine

THE MAN FROM SNOWY RIVER
(Main Title Theme)

Composed and Arranged by
BRUCE ROWLAND

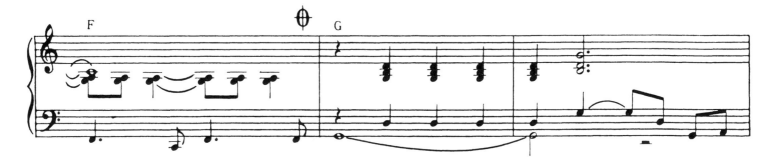

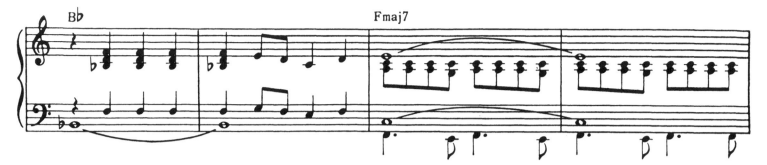

NOW DO WE FIGHT THEM
(Taming The Stallions)

Composed and Arranged by
BRUCE ROWLAND

Moderato

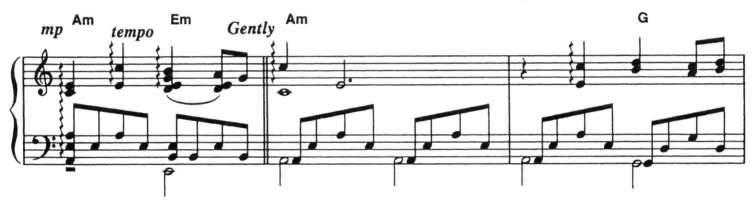

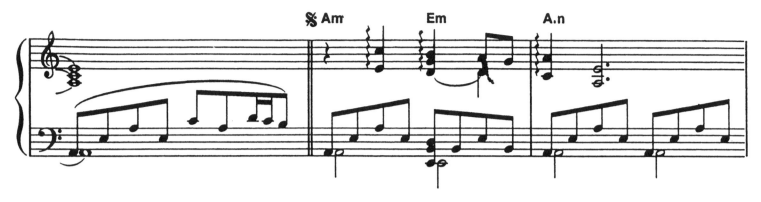

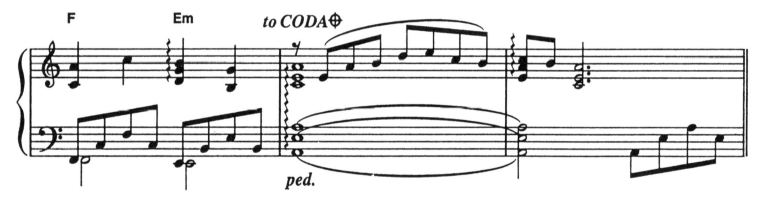

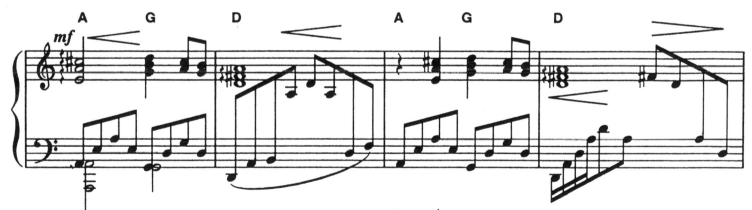

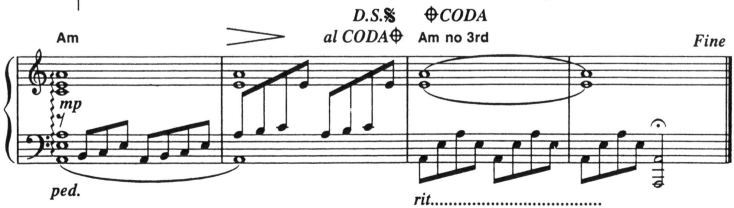